T0182601

Beyond THE

GAME

ATHLETES CHANGE
THE WORLD

PAT TILLMAN

Also by Andrew Maraniss

For Children:

Beyond the Game: Maya Moore

Beyond the Game: LeBron James

For Teens:

Strong Inside (Young Readers Edition): The True Story of How Perry Wallace Broke College Basketball's Color Line

Games of Deception: The True Story of the First U.S. Olympic Basketball Team at the 1936 Olympics in Hitler's Germany

Singled Out: The True Story of Glenn Burke

Inaugural Ballers: The True Story of the First U.S. Women's Olympic Basketball Team

For Adults:

Strong Inside: Perry Wallace and the Collision of Race and Sports in the South

Beyond THE GAME

ATHLETES CHANGE THE WORLD

PAT TILLMAN

by Andrew Maraniss
Illustrated by DeAndra Hodge

VIKING

VIKING

An imprint of Penguin Random House LLC
1745 Broadway, New York, New York 10019

First published in the United States of America by Viking,
an imprint of Penguin Random House LLC, 2024

Text copyright © 2024 by Andrew Maraniss
Illustrations copyright © 2024 by DeAndra Hodge

Visit us online at PenguinRandomHouse.com.

Library of Congress Cataloging-in-Publication Data is available.

ISBN 9780593526217 (hardcover)

ISBN 9780593526224 (paperback)

1st Printing

Printed in the United States of America

LSCC

Edited by Kelsey Murphy
Design by Anabeth Bostrup

Text set in Baskerville

BEYOND THE GAME

A Note about the Series

"A life is not important except in the impact
it has on other lives."
—Jackie Robinson

BEYOND THE GAME tells the stories of remarkable athletes to convey lessons on empathy, justice, and social good. As a parent of elementary-school-age kids, I worry about the profound problems we are leaving for our children to solve. Even concepts as basic as truth and democracy are in peril.

We tend to admire athletes for their strength, speed, and victories. But this series does not celebrate athletes solely for their athletic feats. Instead, it chronicles those who have used their platforms to help other people not merely by writing a check, posing for a photo, or showing up in the community for a day, but through extraordinary acts of courage and selflessness.

Of course, this doesn't mean the subjects of these books are perfect. Athletes are human, after all.

But in a way, that's the point.

The people featured in this series are inspiring not because athletes are more important or better than anyone else, but because in revealing their humanity, they challenge the rest of us to act, too.

"Anytime you have an opportunity to make a difference in this world and you don't, then you are wasting your time on this earth."

—Roberto Clemente

BEYOND THE GAME:

ATHLETES CHANGE THE WORLD

PAT TILLMAN

CHAPTER ONE

FROM THE MOMENT Pat Tillman was born, he moved like he had things to do, places to be, and people to see.

There was a world out there waiting, and he wasn't going to miss a thing.

Even before he could walk, Pat explored. His mom carried him on her back for hikes in the woods near their house in Northern California, pointing out the soaring hawks, slithering snakes, and furry creatures. As they walked, Pat marveled at the freedom of the birds and envied the squirrels that jumped from tree to tree.

Soon, Pat's baby brother Kevin was joining them on their hikes. They were only fourteen months apart—but from the moment Kevin was born, Pat had a best friend and partner in adventure.

Splash!

There went Pat and Kevin, squirting each other with water.

Vroom!

There went Pat and Kevin, playing with their toy cars.

Whoosh!

There went the Tillman boys, scampering through

the woods, leaping from rock to rock.

Dressed only in their superhero underwear, the brothers swung from a rope on their porch, defeating imaginary bad guys.

Pat was a curious, brave, and strong boy. He never stopped talking and asking questions. He loved to learn, and he was ready for school early, starting kindergarten when he was only four years old.

His mom always remembered how prepared and confident Pat was on his first day of kindergarten, even before he left the house. He wolfed down French toast, his favorite breakfast. He put on his new clothes and strapped on his backpack. After his dad snapped a picture by the front door, they drove off to school. Pat was ready for a new world.

The question was whether the world was ready for Pat Tillman.

Long before he became a star football player, and long before he made a courageous choice to enlist in the army at the height of his NFL career, Pat did things his own way. Some people had a hard time figuring him out. But there were two things anyone who ever knew Pat Tillman could agree on: he was a great athlete, and he was a special person well beyond the game.

CHAPTER TWO

PAT'S PARENTS ENCOURAGED him to ask lots of questions. As he grew up, he learned that just because someone was older or more powerful, it did not mean they always had the right answers or did the right thing. Pat was comfortable speaking to adults—and speaking his mind.

At the dinner table, Pat and his family talked about the news in California and around the country.

They talked about politics and sports, about the history of the world and the history of their family.

His mother had grown up near the Civil War battlefield in Gettysburg, Pennsylvania. She told Pat stories about relatives who served in the military. Her father had been a marine in the Korean War; her uncle served in World War II and once parachuted out of a crashing plane; her brother served in Vietnam.

Pat's grandfather on his dad's side was stationed at Pearl Harbor in Hawaii when it was bombed in 1941.

Pat's mom told him that war was a violent and terrible thing that could bring out the best or worst in people, but that soldiers and veterans were to be respected.

In sixth grade, Pat made a presentation on George S. Patton, a famous World War II general. He loved working on projects and writing papers, and he asked *lots* of questions in school.

Pat enjoyed moving from room to room for each subject—each classroom brought new things to learn, a new teacher to question, new kids to meet. If he made a poor grade on a project, he asked his teachers to tell him why. *What didn't you like?* He was always seeking answers, always pressing his teachers to explain their point of view.

But Pat was not perfect. He got into trouble for running and talking in the hallway, wrestling his friends between classes, and jumping across the bleachers in the gym.

When he was seven, Pat joined his first baseball team, and the game taught him valuable lessons about teamwork and self-esteem.

Four years later in the summer of 1988, Pat made a great catch he would remember forever. He had not been playing much in a local tournament. But when the coach put him in a game, Pat made a spectacular diving grab of a ball hit deep into the outfield. He hit and fielded well for the rest of the tournament and came away with something more valuable than a trophy—a jolt of self-confidence that changed his life forever.

CHAPTER THREE

PAT WAS ONLY THIRTEEN when he walked into Leland High School for his first day of classes in the fall of 1990. Standing five feet five and weighing 120 pounds, he didn't look like the greatest athlete in the world.

When he tried out for the varsity baseball team, his coach cut him, saying he needed more experience on the junior varsity. Pat didn't like that idea, so he quit baseball. He told the coach he was going to build muscles and focus on football, a sport he had been playing since seventh grade.

But one of the football coaches told Pat he was making a big mistake. Stick to baseball, he said. The coach saw that Pat was small and young for his grade. Per school rules, he wouldn't even be allowed to join the school's football team until he turned fifteen, toward the end of his sophomore season. Despite all that, Pat disagreed with the coach that playing football was a mistake. He told him that he would work hard enough to become a star on the Leland football team and play in college one day, too.

According to his plan, Pat joined the varsity team when he turned fifteen. And thanks to a growth spurt toward the end of his junior year and long hours in the weight room, Pat grew six inches and gained seventy-five pounds. He still wasn't huge by football standards, but he was big enough to make a difference. By the end of his junior season, he became the team's best player. He was a speedy running back and wide receiver on offense, a punishing linebacker on defense, and a slippery kick returner on special teams. What he lacked in size, Pat made up for in fearlessness, smarts, and hustle.

Pat was a typical teenage boy in some ways, pulling pranks and getting into small fights. But he was different in other ways. He had a soft and thoughtful side—still cherishing a baby pillow his grandmother made him and a blanket he called Fluff. He kept a journal, one time writing about learning to care

Ha!
Ha!
Ha!

more about other people's feelings.

With his concern for others, outgoing personality, and athletic strength, Pat was popular with girls at school. And from his very first day at Leland, he knew he wanted to ask out Marie Ugenti, the beautiful girl from his biology class. But it wasn't until the fall of his senior year, when he was finally taller than Marie, that he first asked her on a date. Pat and Marie were opposites in many ways: he was loud and unconcerned about what other people thought; she was shy and self-conscious. But after their first date at the Crow's Nest restaurant on Santa Cruz Harbor, Pat and Marie were inseparable.

That fall everything was going Pat's way. He had

a new girlfriend, he was making good grades, and his dream of playing college football was still alive.

But then one night he made a terrible mistake.

Pat and Marie were out with a group from their school at a pizza parlor when a classmate burst through the door, shouting that one of their friends was getting beaten up by some other kids. Pat considered himself a protector, so his response was automatic. He ran outside and chased down the person he thought was bullying his friend. He began punching and kicking the boy over and over, hurting him badly.

The whole time, a girl was begging Pat to stop, shouting that he was hitting the wrong guy. But Pat kept going until a police officer arrived. Soon Pat learned that not only had he beaten up someone who had never even thrown a punch, but it was his friend who had started the original fight with another kid in the first place.

Pat broke down crying when he realized what he had done.

Since Pat was seventeen years old and not considered an adult, a judge sentenced him to thirty days in juvenile detention and 250 hours of community service. The punishment caused Pat to think seriously about how he wanted to live his life and how he wanted to treat other people.

Pat was fortunate to receive a second chance. He promised himself he would make better decisions and become more serious about school and football. He realized a mistake—even a really bad one—did not have to define his life. Instead, he would challenge himself to become a better person every day.

CHAPTER FOUR

THERE WERE TIMES when Pat was such a good football player, his coaches would bench him so the other team wouldn't be embarrassed.

In the first half of a playoff game during his senior year, Pat touched the ball six times and scored an incredible four touchdowns. With Pat leading the way, Leland High led 55–0 at halftime. Then Pat ran the second-half kickoff back for another touchdown. That was enough Pat Tillman for one night—he sat on the bench the rest of the game.

After Leland High won the 1993 Central Coast Section championship, it was time for Pat to focus on college. He had been a human highlight machine in high school, but most college coaches thought he was too small and too slow to play at the next level. Pat dreamed of playing at nearby Stanford University, but coaches there weren't interested in him.

Finally, Arizona State, a large school in Tempe, Arizona, that played at the highest level of college football, took a chance on Pat. He accepted the last of the school's twenty-five available scholarships, even though Marie would stay in California for college. Both Pat and Marie agreed that they had made the choices that were best for them—Pat believed ASU was the ideal place to develop as a football player, and Marie thought UC Santa Barbara would offer her a great education.

When he first moved into his dorm at ASU, Pat was so homesick he called home every other day. Adjusting to a new school, harder classes, and the demands of a college football season that started right when he arrived on campus created a lot of stress for him. He missed Marie and his family. Even his mom's first visit was bittersweet because Pat knew eventually she would have to leave. He cried when she said goodbye. As a kid, Pat would climb a tree in his yard when he needed time to sit alone with his thoughts. At ASU, he would climb the two-hundred-foot light towers at Sun Devil Stadium all by himself, finding peace of mind high above campus.

His weekdays were busy from morning until night. He'd wake up before 6:00 a.m. to lift weights and go to class. Then he went to practice, ate dinner, and studied. Saturdays were game days. Whenever he found time, he wrote letters to Marie, attaching interesting articles from the newspaper.

Pat hated the idea of being a "dumb jock," an athlete who didn't care about school. So he worked extra hard, earning a perfect grade point average one semester and eventually graduating in just three and a half years.

His thirst for knowledge wasn't limited to his schoolwork. Walking around campus in old jeans and

sandals, he always clutched a book by his side. He'd even bring one to baseball games to read between innings.

He read great works of fiction, as well as the Bible, the Koran, and the Book of Mormon, even though he wasn't religious. He even read controversial books by dangerous figures like Adolf Hitler. He wanted to stretch his mind, read things he disagreed with, learn history, and force himself to think hard about what he truly believed.

As much as Pat loved to bury his nose in a book, he also loved to be around other people. Nothing made him happier than a good conversation. He enjoyed talking to an ASU tennis player from Hungary about her views of the world. He'd walk into an assistant football coach's office at all hours of the day and night and ask questions about poverty, gay rights, and the beliefs of different religions.

Some people thought it was unusual for a thoughtful, curious, and kind student to be such an aggressive football player. But Pat's close friends knew it all made sense. Pat squeezed every ounce out of every second of his life, whether he was on the field, in the classroom, or striking up a conversation with a stranger.

Pat's energy impressed his Sun Devil teammates. Nobody worked harder, nobody was more fearless, and nobody played with more fire. They called him Hit Man for his ferocious tackling. And he was a smart player, too, able to figure out what the offense was trying to do and arrive at just the right place at just the right time to deliver a bone-crushing tackle.

Over the course of four seasons at Arizona State, Pat steadily increased his role on the team. He improved from a special teams player as a freshman to a defensive substitute as a sophomore, to a starter as a junior, to the Pac-10 Conference's Defensive Player of the Year as a senior in 1997. His team was successful, too. In 1996, the Sun Devils won the Pac-10. Only a loss in the Rose Bowl kept them from winning a national championship. The following season, ASU finished third in the conference and ranked fourteenth nationally.

Pat's teammates loved him, but they had one complaint: Pat flew around making so many tackles, it was sometimes hard for them to get any action!

Pat's doubters had said he would never amount to anything in college ball. By the end of his time in Tempe, he had proven them wrong. But when it came to professional football, most experts thought he had no chance. They said he was too small and too slow. When the NFL hosted the best college players at a workout before the 1998 draft, they didn't even invite Pat. It wasn't the first time he had been underestimated, and he was determined not to give up hope.

On April 18 and 19, 1998, all thirty NFL teams gathered in New York for their annual draft. Each year, NFL teams take turns adding to their rosters by selecting the best college players. But none of the teams called Pat's name in the first, second, third, fourth, fifth, or sixth rounds. Maybe the experts were right. Maybe Pat would never play pro ball. Then finally in the seventh and final round, with the 226th pick of the draft (out of a total of 241), the Arizona Cardinals selected Pat. They offered him the least amount of money allowed by NFL rules. Still, Pat had achieved the near impossible: he was officially a professional football player.

At least for training camp.

CHAPTER FIVE

WHEN PAT ARRIVED at Arizona Cardinals train-ing camp, his new teammates took one look at his long blond hair and started calling him Goldilocks. It wasn't exactly the most intimidating nickname for a football player. As a seventh-round pick and one of the smaller players on the field, Pat knew he was not guaranteed a place on the team. He was going to have to stand out for more than his hair if he wanted a spot on the roster once the regular season started.

By the first day of camp, he had memorized the playbook so he would know exactly what to do. He wouldn't make any careless rookie mistakes. And while other defenders took it easy on their teammates in practice, Pat tackled them as hard as he could.

His coaches loved his energy, and when it was time for the Cardinals' first game of the 1998 season, Pat had earned a starting position. This was a rare feat for a rookie drafted in the seventh round. Over the season, Pat started ten games and made seventy-three tackles, the fourth most on the team. His strong play helped lead the Cardinals to the playoffs and a first-round victory over the Dallas Cowboys, the team's first playoff win since 1947.

But sometimes progress doesn't follow a straight line. Pat's second season, in 1999, was a disappointment. The team lost ten of its sixteen games, and Pat lost his starting job. He knew that if he didn't come back better than ever for the 2000 season, his career might be over.

Once again, Pat chose to do things differently.

In the most important offseason of his life, he tried two things he'd never done before: exploring Europe with Marie and running his first marathon. He approached the trip overseas with the curiosity of a puppy. He sampled every sausage he could find in Germany and every pastry in France. He chatted with fishermen, tourists, and baristas. He woke up early and ran through ancient streets to stay in shape and wrote his thoughts in a journal each night before bed.

When the vacation was over, he ran a marathon in California, recording a time of three hours and forty-eight minutes. One hundred and sixty-nine runners placed ahead of him, but Pat didn't mind. He was proud that he competed and finished all 26.2 miles. He was the only NFL player to run a marathon all year.

Pat completed the offseason by lifting weights and shedding extra pounds, arriving at training camp in the best shape of his life. He had more confidence than ever, and he believed he could be a star in the NFL. All he had to do was prove it.

And.

He.

Did.

All season long, when the other team ran the ball, Pat made the tackle.

When they passed the ball, Pat made the tackle.

Crunch. Bang. Boom.

Tackle. Tackle. Tackle.

By season's end, Tillman led the team with 155 tackles from the strong safety position. A writer from *Sports Illustrated* called him one of the best players in the NFL.

After a season like that, it was no surprise that other teams wanted Pat to play for them.

The St. Louis Rams offered him a five-year contract worth nearly $10 million, a lot more than the $512,000 the Cardinals paid him.

For Pat, the decision was easy.

He turned the Rams down. Once again, he did what he thought was right, even if it wasn't the popular choice.

Loyalty mattered to Pat. The Cardinals were the team that had drafted him. His coaches believed in him. And Pat relished the challenge of playing for an underdog like Arizona. St. Louis had won the Super Bowl two years earlier. Playing for them would be taking the easy way out. Nothing with the Cardinals was easy.

Money wasn't the most important thing to Pat anyway. He felt uneasy that professional athletes made high salaries when other people worked hard for not much money at all. While his teammates bought fancy cars, he drove a used station wagon. He and Marie lived in a small, simple house. When they went to Europe, they didn't jet around from one swanky hotel to the next; they rode trains and backpacked to hostels.

Pat was different from a lot of his teammates in other ways, too. When he stayed up late, it wasn't to head to the clubs and party; it was to have friends over to talk. He loved to drink coffee and tea. He had two cats. And he didn't believe in God, so when his teammates gathered to pray, he stood off to the side. He knew that being religious doesn't make a person good or bad: it's how you live your life and treat other people that matters.

He kept every letter that fans mailed him, studied for a master's degree in history during the offseason, and never bragged about playing pro ball. When strangers asked him what he did for living, he'd make up a job that sounded boring. Pat was no ordinary pro athlete.

But that didn't mean Pat ever took anything for granted. He constantly tested his body and his mind. A marathon one year, a triathlon the next. A new book, a new argument, a new subject to study. One of his favorite quotes was from the writer Ralph Waldo Emerson: "The world belongs to the energetic."

With that motto as his guide, Pat believed taking risks was necessary in order to become a better person.

And just a few weeks into the 2001 season, he started thinking about making his most surprising decision yet.

CHAPTER SIX

PAT WAS STILL in bed when his phone rang early on a Tuesday morning in September 2001. It was his brother Kevin telling him to get up and turn on the TV.

Pat was horrified by what he saw: planes crashing into the World Trade Center in New York, the two enormous towers burning and crumbling to the ground.

The deadly act of terrorism on September 11, 2001, shook the country and stirred patriotic feelings in many Americans. Pat thought about his relatives who'd defended the country during times of war. Playing football didn't feel very important in comparison.

On October 7, as Pat prepared for a game against the Philadelphia Eagles, President George W. Bush appeared on the stadium's video board, announcing the US had launched attacks against terrorists in Afghanistan. The nation was at war. Across the country, some people blamed all Muslims for the terrorists' actions, as if the men who committed the violent attacks on the US represented a worldwide religion of nearly two billion people. When some

Americans responded to the terrorists' violence with hate or violence of their own against innocent people because of their religion, it made Pat uncomfortable.

And as the season progressed, something else bothered him. Pat heard other NFL players talking about their outrage over the 9/11 attacks and their support for the war. But as far as he knew, none of them planned to leave their careers in the NFL or take any other action. Pat believed people needed to do much more than talk. He asked himself what he was willing to sacrifice to defend his country.

One night, he climbed into bed with a question for Marie, who was nearly asleep. Before the season had started, Pat proposed marriage to Marie and she said yes. Now he surprised her with an entirely different question: "What if I joined the army?"

It was a question thousands of other couples discussed, but this was different. Pat was a professional football player at the height of his career, engaged to the woman he loved, looking at a new contract worth more than $3 million. Life was good—and comfortable. Why even think about giving that up?

But money, fame, and comfort didn't mean as much to Pat as honor, courage, and sacrifice. If America needed defending, why rely on someone else to do it? If this was an important moment in history, how could he not be a part of it?

On May 4, 2002, Pat married Marie in a simple outdoor ceremony. Before the newlyweds left for a honeymoon in Bora Bora, Pat, along with his brother

Kevin, walked into a recruiting office in Arizona and enlisted in the army. Pat and Kevin set their sights on the Rangers, an elite group of special forces. Pat's pro football career, at least temporarily, was over.

He wasn't a strong safety with a fat contract anymore. He was a soldier with a salary of less than $1,300 per month.

Pat began to realize how silly it was when football players talked about games as if they were battles. His "opponents" now wouldn't be trying to run past him for touchdowns. They would be trying to kill him.

CHAPTER SEVEN

WHEN WORD GOT out that Pat Tillman, NFL star, had joined the army, people working for President Bush wanted to make a big deal about it. They thought it would make good publicity for the war. TV and newspaper reporters wanted to talk to Pat about his decision. They knew it would make a popular story.

But Pat refused to speak about his decision publicly. He hadn't joined the military to get attention.

All he wanted was to be a good soldier.

The first step was basic training, a challenging ten-week course that prepares new enlistees for army life. Pat knew it would be hard, but he expected to be surrounded by other people with high ideals just like him. Instead, he was disappointed to discover that many of the soldiers around him joined the army as simply another way to make a living. Some of these new recruits had few choices in life. Others were aimless young adults who had squandered opportunities. Regardless, Pat was upset when the recruits acted immature, whined, or avoided hard work. Some of his fellow soldiers were jealous that Pat was a football star; others said he was dumb to leave the NFL.

Getting used to his new teammates was one

thing. Army rules were another. Pat understood there were lots of rules and obligations in the army and he respected them. But that didn't mean he liked them. All the saluting, the time spent mowing lawns and polishing equipment, the expectation that he would never question his superiors or speak his mind; it was all frustrating. He was itching to do more.

On top of all that, he missed Marie so much it hurt. When he called her, the sound of her voice made him cry. He wrote in his journal, asking what made him walk away from a life that most people would envy.

But he also believed that the pain he felt was good for him. Life was about sensations and emotions. Happy and sad moments were both important. The hard times made him appreciate the good ones.

His army experience would make him a better man and husband.

Pat did everything that was asked of him by his superiors—and more—and he treated everyone like they mattered, regardless of their rank. One time during a drill on the shooting range, Pat saw a soldier struggling in the mud, so he stopped what he was doing to encourage him.

Pat had mixed feelings about the guns he and the other soldiers were learning to fire. He knew guns were necessary in the army, but he didn't obsess over them like some of the others. And he feared some soldiers were too careless to use them properly.

On a tragic day two years later, his fears were proven right.

CHAPTER EIGHT

SOLDIERS UNDERSTAND THEY must obey an order, whether they agree with it or not. So when Pat and Kevin learned their unit was headed to Iraq in March 2003, they went without complaint, even though they did not support the war.

The whole reason they enlisted in the army was to go after the terrorists in Afghanistan who led the September 11 attacks. Now they were being asked to fight in a war that, they believed, had nothing to do with September 11 and would do the most harm to ordinary Iraqi people who wanted to live in peace. The Tillmans were not alone in their opposition. The leader of the United Nations deemed the war "illegal," and even US intelligence agencies discredited President Bush's rationales for it.

Marie felt the same way as the Tillman brothers. One day after Pat and Kevin departed together for the Middle East, Marie drove past an anti-war demonstration near Fort Lewis, Washington, where she lived. She was tempted to join it, but she believed getting involved might cause a scene and make things more difficult for Pat.

Just as Marie kept her feelings to herself, Pat knew

that as a professional soldier, he had to put his personal feelings aside and do his job. The problem was, once he got to Iraq, he had very little to do. He mostly sat around doing nothing. Even though he disagreed with the war, if he was going to be sent halfway around the world, he at least wanted to feel useful.

He kept busy by reading books, staying up late making coffee and talking with friends in his unit, writing letters to Marie, and imagining their future together. When he joined the army, he thought he would be fighting for a good cause, which would make up for their time apart. But now he felt like a fool for leaving her. He comforted himself with visions of their future children, of school plays and ball games and family road trips.

Finally, after five weeks, he and Kevin were sent home. The brothers had avoided much danger; Pat had fired his gun just one time, and that was only a warning shot to get some cars to move.

When he arrived back in Washington, Pat heard surprising news. The Seattle Seahawks wanted to sign him. The team believed it could get Pat out of the army early since he had served overseas. Once again, Pat refused to take the easy way out. He had promised the army he would serve for three years, and he wanted to honor that commitment. The NFL could wait.

Back at Fort Lewis, Pat was now an experienced soldier. When new Rangers arrived, he didn't act like he was better than them. Instead, he treated them with respect, asked about their families, and helped them fit in. Pat felt more at peace with his decision to join the military than ever before. The experience had made him a more well-rounded, humble, grateful person.

After less than a year back home, Pat and Kevin found out their unit was being deployed to Afghanistan, where they had wanted to be all along. One of their jobs would be to sweep through small villages, searching for enemy fighters and weapons.

It was dangerous, stressful work even on a good day.

And then on one tragic afternoon, everything went wrong.

CHAPTER NINE

SOMETIMES THE STORY of how a soldier was killed begins with something as ordinary as a broken fuel pump. That's what happened on April 22, 2004.

A Humvee wouldn't move, and that was a big problem. The soldiers couldn't fix it on the spot, and they couldn't just leave it there to be captured by enemy fighters. Somehow, Pat's unit had to move the truck out of a remote, mountainous

region of Afghanistan to get it fixed.

First Lieutenant David Uthlaut called for a heli-copter to fly in and scoop up the broken-down vehicle, but his superiors denied his request. Instead, they ordered him to split up his unit: half of them needed to drive to the Afghan village of Manah by sundown to look for enemy fighters and weapons; the other half would tow the truck to a repair site.

Uthlaut knew it was dangerous to split his platoon in half and travel through dangerous territory in day-light. Both decisions made his soldiers more likely to be ambushed. But once again, his commanders didn't listen to his warnings. So he did what he was told and split them up.

Pat was in the first group of nineteen Rangers,

known as Serial 1, bound for Manah. They drove slowly through a series of canyons so tall and narrow their trucks could barely squeeze through. After realizing they had missed a turn, they pulled over to the side of the dirt road.

Behind them, Kevin Tillman and Serial 2 were supposed to be going a different direction to escort the damaged Humvee to the highway. But the twisting roads were too hard for the tow truck to navigate. So they turned around and drove back the other way, in the same direction as Pat and Serial 1.

Suddenly there was an explosion and confusion— and the men in Serial 2 began shooting their guns toward the top of the canyon.

Pat heard the commotion and bravely sprinted

toward Serial 2, ready to help his friends. He was followed by an eighteen-year-old Ranger named Bryan O'Neal and an Afghan ally named Sayed Farhad.

Shockingly, members of Serial 2 mistakenly started firing at Pat, Bryan, and Sayed.

Pat couldn't believe what was happening, and Kevin was too far back to see that his brother was in danger.

Pat waved his arms and shouted: "Stop! Friendlies!"

The shooting stopped. Pat believed the gunners had realized their carelessness.

But then the shooting started again.

Pat relied on his training and did what he was supposed to in a situation like this: he threw a purple smoke grenade to identify himself as an American soldier. But the shooters didn't pay any attention, and they kept firing.

The men shooting at him were only around forty yards away, roughly the distance between home plate and second base on a Major League field.

"Cease fire! Friendlies! I am Pat Tillman!" he shouted. "I am Pat Tillman!"

But his pleas went unanswered.

Pat Tillman was shot and killed by his fellow soldiers.

It was the result of a horrible series of mistakes and bad decisions.

And the army was about to make things worse, misleading Pat's family and the American public about how Pat was killed.

CHAPTER TEN

ON MAY 3, 2004, Pat's family and friends gathered at the San Jose Municipal Rose Garden for his memorial service. It was the same location where Pat had celebrated his high school graduation—and it was just one day before what would have been his second wedding anniversary.

ESPN aired the service live on TV, and sports figures and politicians joined members of Pat's family

in delivering remarks. They shared stories about a remarkable athlete who proved that life was about way more than sports.

Sports radio host Jim Rome said that we often call talented athletes "heroes and warriors, when in reality they are neither." But Pat, he said, was someone to admire, not for his football stats, but for his "hunger, desire, courage, competitive spirit, integrity, honesty, selflessness, the things that make you a great athlete and a great man."

Quarterback Jake Plummer, Pat's teammate at Arizona State and with the Cardinals, referred to the fact that Pat had once been named to a magazine's list of "50 Most Beautiful People." Beauty, Jake said, was not about a pretty face or a nice smile.

"To me, beauty is living life to higher standards, stronger morals and ethics and believing in them, whether people tell you you're right or wrong," he said. "Beauty is not wasting a day . . . Beauty is being real, being genuine . . . Beauty is expanding your mind, always seeking knowledge, not being content, always going after something and challenging yourself. Beauty is red, white, and blue with stars and stripes, and beauty is why we're here today. Pat was one of the most beautiful people to have ever entered my life."

A military officer also spoke, telling a story about how Pat died that simply was not true. He implied that Pat had been killed by the enemy while sacrificing himself to save the lives of other American soldiers. The made-up story was part of a campaign to hide the truth and build support for the war.

There's an old saying that the truth is the first thing to die in any war, and here was a prime example. Political and military leaders felt it would be embarrassing to admit Pat was killed by his own men.

So they made up a story to tell Pat's grieving family and the media. And they ordered the soldiers who were there in Afghanistan and saw what really happened to repeat the lie. They even lied to Pat's brother Kevin, who was there but had not seen Pat get killed and didn't know the truth.

But the truth can't stay hidden forever. Gradually, tiny bits of the real story bubbled to the surface. Over the course of years, Pat's family, especially his mom, demanded full answers about what really happened and why it was covered up. Eventually, after persistent questions from the family and multiple congressional hearings, the truth came out. It became clear that the army and government lied about Pat's death in order to generate positive publicity for the war. Marie said that the way the military handled Pat's death went "against everything he stood for."

It was all so disrespectful.

And unnecessary.

No matter how Pat was killed, he was still a hero.

"The bottom line is the American people are capable of determining their own ideals for heroes," said army veteran Jessica Lynch. "They don't need to be told elaborate lies . . . The truth of war is not always easy. The truth is always more heroic than the hype."

CHAPTER ELEVEN

PAT TILLMAN WAS an extraordinary football player. The energy he carried onto the field inspired his teammates and his fans. But Pat's influence and interests extended well beyond the game.

If he saw a problem, he didn't stand around waiting for someone else to solve it. He took responsibility and jumped into the action. He formed his own opinions, challenged other people to defend theirs, and was not afraid to change his mind. He wanted to learn as much as he could, experience as much of the world as possible, and stand up for what he thought was right.

This approach to life is what led him from the NFL to the army. Pat's death was tragic, but he is not forgotten. Today, people honor him in many different ways.

At the ESPN "ESPY Awards" each year, the Pat Tillman Award is given to someone connected to sports who has served others in a special way. Outside the Arizona Cardinals' stadium, a five-hundred-pound bronze sculpture of Pat faces a reflecting pool. At Arizona State University, the Pat Tillman Veterans Center helps former soldiers and their families.

In his hometown of New Almaden, California, a marker outside Pat's favorite park remembers him as a "voracious reader, inquisitive scholar, civic volunteer, aggressive athlete and a patriotic and self-less soldier."

Pat's legacy continues in another important way. In 2004, Marie created the Pat Tillman Foundation to support veterans with a passion for helping other people. The foundation provides college scholarships to assist people who "lead through action," just like Pat.

These Tillman Scholars, now numbering more than eight hundred, are living proof of something Pat once said: "Somewhere inside, we hear a voice. It leads us in the direction of the person we wish to become. But it is up to us whether or not to follow."

Most people will never play professional football or serve in the military. But we can all learn from the way Pat Tillman lived with purpose, curiosity, and courage.

What direction does the voice in your head lead you?

LEARNING FROM PAT TILLMAN: HOW WILL YOU HELP OTHERS?

1. Pat Tillman was curious about the world. He challenged himself to keep learning new things, read interesting books, and debate ideas with people who might disagree with him.

   • How can you be like Pat in this way?

2. Pat proved wrong coaches who thought he was too small and too slow to play football in high school, college, and the professionals. How do you respond when people doubt your abilities?

   • What can you learn from how Pat dealt with his doubters?

3. One of Pat's favorite quotes was "the world belongs to the energetic."

   • What does this mean to you? How can you put this idea into action?

4. Pat learned a lot from his terrible mistake in high school when he hurt an innocent person.

  • Have you ever learned something from a mistake? How did learning that lesson make you a better person?

5. How will you honor Pat Tillman's memory in the way you live your life?

EXTRAS

FIFTEEN PRO ATHLETES WHO SERVED IN THE MILITARY

Name	Sport	Military Service
Grover Cleveland Alexander	MLB	Army, World War I
Chuck Bednarik	NFL	Army Air Corps, World War II
Yogi Berra	MLB	Navy, World War II
Rocky Bleier	NFL	Army, Vietnam
Roberto Clemente	MLB	Marines
Bob Feller	MLB	Navy, World War II
Hank Greenberg	MLB	Army Air Corps, World War II
Tim James	NBA	Army, Iraq
Joe Louis	Boxing	Army, World War II
Willie Mays	MLB	Army, Korea
Phil Rizzuto	MLB	Navy, World War II
David Robinson	NBA	Navy
Jackie Robinson	MLB	Army
Warren Spahn	MLB	Army, World War II
Ted Williams	MLB	Marines, World War II and Korea

PAT TILLMAN'S COLLEGE FOOTBALL ACCOLADES

2010	College Football Hall of Fame inductee
2008	Arizona State Hall of Fame inductee
1997	All-American
1997	Sporting News Honda Scholar Athlete of the Year
1997	Pac-10 Defensive Player of the Year
1997, 1996	GTE District VIII Academic All-American
1997, 1996	Academic All-Pac-10

PAC-10 CONFERENCE IN 1997

University Nickname	Location
Arizona Wildcats	Tucson
Arizona State Sun Devils	Tempe
California Golden Bears	Berkeley
UCLA Bruins	Los Angeles
USC Trojans	Los Angeles
Oregon Ducks	Eugene
Oregon State Beavers	Corvallis
Stanford Cardinal	Stanford, CA
Washington Huskies	Seattle
Washington State Cougars	Pullman

PAT'S ARIZONA CARDINALS (NFL) STATISTICS

Year	Age	G	GS	I	IY	FF	FR	Sacks	Tackles
1998	22	16	10	0	0	0	0	1.0	73
1999	23	16	1	2	7	1	1	0.0	52
2000	24	16	16	1	30	0	2	1.5	155
2001	25	12	12	0	0	0	0	0	94
Total	N/A	60	39	3	37	1	3	2.5	374

*Games * Games Started * Interceptions * Interception Yards * Fumbles Forced * Fumble Recoveries*

Source: Pro Football Reference

ESPN PAT TILLMAN AWARD "ESPY" HONOREES

Year	Name	Achievement
2014	Joshua Sweeney	US Paralympic gold medalist (hockey) and Purple Heart recipient
2015	Danielle Green	Notre Dame basketball player and Purple Heart recipient
2016	Elizabeth Marks	US Army sergeant and Invictus Games gold medalist
2017	Israel Del Toro	Invictus Games gold medalist and Purple Heart recipient
2018	Jake Wood	Navy and Marine Corps Commendation Medal recipient
2019	Kirstie Ennis	Marine and founder of Kirstie Ennis Foundation
2020	Kim Clavel	Health care worker and boxing champion
2021	Marcus Rashford	Manchester United soccer player
2022	Gretchen Evans	Army command sergeant major and founder of Team UNBROKEN
2023	Buffalo Bills Training Staff	Saved life of Bills safety Damar Hamlin

GLOSSARY

Afghanistan: Mountainous country in western Asia. Capital: Kabul.

Army Rangers: Combat experts who specialize in conducting raids in enemy territory. Formally known as the 75th Ranger Regiment.

Basic training: Also known as boot camp. Ten-week program that prepares new military recruits for the physical and mental demands of service.

Community service: Unpaid work for the betterment of others.

Ralph Waldo Emerson: Nineteenth-century American essayist and philosopher from Massachusetts.

Ethics: Moral principles that guide a person's behavior and understanding of right and wrong.

Friendly fire: Term that refers to the firing of weapons from one's own side in a battle, especially when it results in injury or death.

Humvee: Nickname for a high-mobility multipurpose wheeled vehicle, a common four-wheel drive military truck.

Iraq: Country in Southwest Asia, centered in the Tigris-Euphrates basin. Capital: Baghdad.

Pearl Harbor: US naval base in Hawaii that was the site of a Japanese attack on December 7, 1941, leading the United States into World War II.

Veteran: Person who has served in the military.

RESOURCES FOR FAMILIES

Where Men Win Glory: The Odyssey of Pat Tillman by Jon Krakauer

The Letter: My Journey Through Love, Loss, and Life by Marie Tillman

Boots on the Ground by Dusk: My Tribute to Pat Tillman by Mary Tillman

Kevin Tillman's essay in *Paths of Dissent: Soldiers Speak Out Against America's Misguided Wars*

The Tillman Story documentary

Pat Tillman Foundation website: PatTillmanFoundation.org

Pat Tillman Veterans Center website: Veterans.ASU.edu

AUTHOR BIO

New York Times bestselling author **ANDREW MARANISS** writes sports- and social justice-related nonfiction for children, teens, and adults. His bestselling adult book, *Strong Inside*, received the Lillian Smith Book Award and the RFK Book Awards' Special Recognition Prize. The middle grade adaptation was named a Book of the Year by the ALA. His next YA book, *Games of Deception*, received the Sydney Taylor Book Honor.

His YA biography *Singled Out* was named one of the 100 Best Baseball Books Ever Written by *Esquire* and was a Rainbow Book List selection. His latest YA book, *Inaugural Ballers*, was a *School Library Journal* Book of the Year.

You can visit Andrew Maraniss at AndrewMaraniss.com or follow him on Facebook @AndrewMaranissAuthor, on Twitter @TruBlu24, and on Instagram @AMaraniss.

AND STAY TUNED FOR WHAT'S NEXT:

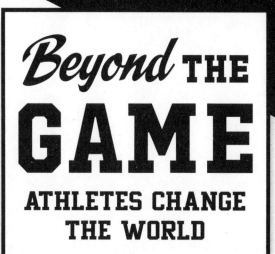

Beyond THE
GAME
ATHLETES CHANGE
THE WORLD

JORDAN MARIE BRINGS THREE WHITE HORSES WHETSTONE

COMING IN SUMMER 2025!